Let's Read Dashavatar Tales

Creative Editor
Vinnie Mathur

Designed by
Bhupender Singh

Retold by
Kiren Babal

Galgotia Publications pvt. ltd.

Edition 2009

ISBN:- 978-81-7515-689-0

Published by Suneel Galgotia for Galgotia Publications Pvt. Ltd.,
5, Ansari Road, Darya Ganj, New Delhi-110 002

Galgotia Publications pvt. ltd.

Contents

Holy Trinity

In Hindu mythology, Lord Vishnu is the preserver of the Universe. Lord Brahma, the creator, is considered self-born from the lotus, which grew from the navel of Vishnu. Along with Shiva, who is the destroyer, they are known to be three primary Gods. Together they make the Holy Trinity.

Lord Vishnu is considered to be the Supreme Personality of Godhead by Vaishnavas. Vishnu is the cosmic ocean which spreads everywhere before the creation of the Universe.

He is also called

Narayana, representing Himself in the human form, sleeping on the coiled serpent, Sheshnaag. His carrier is Garuda, who is half-bird (eagle) and half-man.

Lord Vishnu usually has four hands. His one hand holds a conch shell (shankh), second holds a wheel (chakra), third holds a club (gada), and the fourth hand holds a lotus flower (padma).

He has blue com- plexion

and wears yellow garments.

He also wears a jewel, Kaustubha on His chest. The club and the wheel are the Lord's symbols of punishment for the demons and miscreants. The lotus and the conch shell are used to bless the devotees.

Lord Vishnu has often taken human forms or the Avatars, to bless all His devotees.

Dashavatar (ten incarnations) is the story of the Avatars of Lord Vishnu, who came down on Earth to kill the demons and protect His devotees from danger, and thus, ensuring the victory of good over evil.

Lord Vishnu declared, "Whenever and wherever there is a decline in religious practice, and a predominant rise of irreligion, O descendants of Bharat! At that time I descend myself." The Vedas (Principles of religion) resided in the mouth of Lord Brahma. It is understood that the Vedas were the words spoken by Lord Himself to Brahma, from within His heart. And Brahma performed His role through the Vedas.

गुरुर् ब्रह्मा गुरुर् विष्णुः गुरुर् देवो महेश्वराः।
गुरुः साक्षात् परंब्रह्मा तस्मै श्री गुरवे नमः।।

Guru is verily the representative of Brahma, Vishnu and Shiva. He creates, sustains knowledge and destroys the weeds of ignorance. I salute such a Guru!

Matsya Avatar

One day as Lord Brahma was relaxing, the Vedas happened to slip out of His mouth. A demon, Hayagriva came and saw Brahma relaxing, "Wow! The Lord is sleeping, I can steal the Vedas easily." Saying so, he stole the Vedas, absorbed them

in his mouth and hid in the deeper depths of the ocean. Filled with remorse, Brahma implored Vishnu, "Please get back the Vedas from the demon, otherwise the whole world will be destroyed."

Vishnu assured him, "O Lord! Don't panic, I will retrieve the Vedas from him." He looked around and saw King Satyavrata who was offering prayers on the bank of a holy river. Lord Vishnu decided to take the form of a fish. When the king took some water from the river, he saw a tiny fish with

a horn in his cupped hands. He was about to put it back in the water when to his sur-

prise, the fish spoke, "O noble soul, please don't throw me into the water... Big creatures might swallow me up... I have come to you for shelter."

Amazed,

the king put it in his kamandala (pot) and brought it into his palace. By the time he got home, the fish had already become bigger, so he put it in a big jar. The

fish immediately expanded its body and became too big for the jug. He then placed it in a large vessel but to his amazement, the fish grew bigger and bigger. From vessel to the pond, to lake, and then the largest lake. Finally, the king placed the fish in the ocean, but it went on asking for more space. Satyavrata became suspicious,

"How can a fish grow so big in one day that it overgrows the largest ocean? It must be some divine form." He pleaded, "O Lord! Please appear before us." As Lord Vishnu revealed His true form, the sky lit up with a bright flash of light and a voice echoed, "Satyavrata, as a noble soul, you are chosen for a big task."

"Lord, I am honoured to be at your service!" the king's voice cracked with joy.

"After seven days, the ocean will rise and engulf the entire world," the voice echoed, "You must build a large ship and put the saintly people (seven sages) and a pair of each living creature in it. Only the ship and its inhabitants will be saved."

"But Lord!" the king asked, "How will the ship survive the mighty flood?"

"You must tie it to the horn of the fish and it shall be guided to safety!" came the voice.
The king took to the task hurriedly.

Lord Vishnu as Matsya Avtar, in all its enormity dived into the depths of the ocean where Hay-agriva was hiding. In the fierce duel that followed Hayagriva was killed and the 'Vedas' retreived for the next spell of creation.

After a week, the darkness crept in, ocean rose and a devastating flood drowned everything on the Earth except the ship and its inhabitants. It was tied to the horn of the fish using Vasuki, the snake as a rope. King Satyavrata then offered prayers to Lord Vishnu. The Lord appeared and taught him and the saintly persons Vedic knowledge.

As the water receded, life began afresh, wiping out all the evil.

आदिमत्स्यः स जयताद्यः श्वासोच्छ्वासितैर्जलैः ।
गगने विद्धेम्भोधिं गगनं च महोदधौ ।।

First of all, Matsya Avtara of Lord Vishnu be victorious, who spraying the water by his inhale exhale, created ocean in the sky and sky in the ocean.(a new spell of creation.)

Kurma Avatar

The second incarnation of Vishnu is Kurma, a tortoise. The myth of Kurma belongs to the story of Samudra Manthan (Churning of the Ocean). Indra, the Lord of Heaven was offered a garland by Sage Durvasa. Instead of wearing it, Indra hung it on the tusk of his elephant, Airawat, who trampled it. Enraged, the sage cursed, "Proud Indra! You and your accomplices shall lose all the divine powers." Soon enough, the demon King Bali defeated the Gods in a battle.

Ashamed and filled with remorse, Indra and the Gods pleaded before Lord Brahma, "Please help us regain our power and dignity again." Brahma sent them to Lord Vishnu who told them, "The only way to restore your immortality is to drink Amrit (the magic nectar) from the Kalash, lying at the bottom of the ocean... And for this you will have to churn the ocean."

"But that is a mighty task," cried the Gods, "How will we ever do it?"

Lord Vishnu advised, "Ask for the demons' support. They will surely agree if you share the Amrit with them." The demons agreed and it was decided that they would hold the hood of the snake, and the Gods, the tail. Thus, began the preparation for churning of the ocean. The great mountain Mandara was used as a pole to stir the water, and the serpent Vasuki, as a rope to move it.

As the churning began, the pressure on the snake's hood increased. It began spitting venom, killing many demons. The churning brought out many things from the womb of the ocean. The first thing to come out was a fatal poison or Halahal, which was capable of destroying all living creatures.

Lord Shiva appeared and swallowed all the poison. He kept it in His throat and that is how He came to be known as Neelkantha or the blue-throated one. Yet another problem cropped up with the churning. The Gods cried in despair, "Lord! Help, help... The mountain is sinking." Lord Vishnu who was carefully watching the whole incident, immediately reincarnated as Kurma.

He held the mountain on His mighty back and the churning continued.

Many valuables emerged from the depths of the sea: the Kamdhenu, a wish fulfilling cow; Laxmi, the goddess of wealth; Kalpavriksha, the wish fulfilling tree etc. Finally, after great effort, the Amrit Kalash, emerged from the vast ocean.

"Run, run, catch it," cried the demons.

As the Gods and the demons tussled for the Kalash, a golden light flashed and there stood Mohini, the heart charmer. All the men bedazzled and stared at the beauty. Taking away the Kalash, Mohini said, "Sit and I shall serve the nectar." Then dancing and singing, she served Amrit to the Gods first.

The demons, Rahu and Ketu noticed, "Let's sit amongst the Gods." They managed to get a drop of Amrit. The Sun and the Moon Gods immediately shouted, "They are demons — Rahu and Ketu."

Mohini at once, threw the Kalash on Vishnu's chariot, the Garuda, and came into the true form.

She was Vishnu Himself; He charged His Sudarshan Chakra at the daring demons. Their heads separated from their bodies, but the effect of Amrit had made their heads immortal.

Spinning around the Sun and the Moon Gods, Rahu and Ketu cried aloud, "We shall cross your path every year. It will be most inauspicious to see you at that time."

As Lord Vishnu boarded His chariot with the Kalash, the demons chased after him. In the tussle, a few drops of Amrit fell at Ujjain, Nasik, Allahabad and Haridwar. According to popular belief, devotees gather in these places to wash off their sins by taking a dip in the holy waters. The Kumbh Melas are organised in these places, every twelfth year.

इति स भगवान्विष्णुः कूर्माकृतिर्धृतभूधरः
सुरहितविधौ बद्धश्रद्धः सुधां विदधेम्बुधेः।

Containing Mount Mandara on his mighty back, reincarnated in the form of Kurma, Lord Vishnu obtained Amrit from the depth of sea, to serve the dedicated demigods.

Varaha Avatar

Lord Vishnu, in His third incarnation, appeared as a giant boar to save the Earth and kill the demon, Hiranyaksha. Once Hiranyaksha took penance and meditated intensely. As his devotion reached

Brahma, He was forced to appear, "My child! Open your eyes and ask for your wish."

Hiranyaksha opened his eyes and said, "My Lord! Grant me that no God, demon, beast or man can ever kill me."

"So it shall be," Brahma said and disappeared.

Vain-glorious, he announced, "Now Gods can't defeat me and nobody can stop me from ruling all the three worlds." Hiranyaksha invaded Heaven, defeated Indra and the other Gods. They took shelter in the caves of the mountain ranges on Earth. In a fit of pride one day, Hiranyaksha hid the Earth under the sea and challenged, "All those who call themselves the God, show up and save the Earth, Ha... ha... ha..."

The Gods were alarmed and rushed to Vishnu, "Please help, Mother Earth has to be rescued." Lord Vishnu transformed into a tiny boar. In seconds that creature grew and grew, till it was the size of a large mountain.

Emitting a terrifying roar, it took one mighty leap into the air, tore the clouds with its hoofs and then dived with mighty strength at the bottom of the ocean in search of Mother Earth. Reaching the other end of the ocean, it discovered the Earth, sad and forlorn.

The boar dug his tusk into the ocean-bed, lifted Mother Earth onto it, and brought it to the surface.

Hiranyaksha rushed towards the boar challenging, "You fraudulent fellow! Coward... Return me my Earth or I'll crush your head." Saying so, the demon snatched the

Earth from the boar. The Varaha charged at the demon instantly. They fought fiercely for hours. Fearing sunset, Brahma warned Varaha, "You've only an hour before the sunset. Destroy the demon before it's

dark, or the demon will resort to black magic." Hearing this, the Varaha hit the demon with a deadly blow on his face with His fist and tossed him in the air. He fell on his head with a crash and died on the spot.

Thus, Lord Vishnu brought the Earth to the surface to support life once again.

आशाकाशप्रसृत्तवपुषा व्याप्तसप्ताब्धिलोकः
स्तोकारम्भक्षुभितभुवन भ्रंशशंकानिलीनः।
स्वस्थां धृत्वा स्थिरनिजपदे क्ष्मां हिरण्याक्षमुग्रं
क्रोडीकृत्य प्रसभमवधीत्क्रीडया क्रोडराजः।।

Varaha avtar Lord Vishnu ,established the earth in its safe place,then noosed the arrogant Hiranyaksh in his armpit, killing effortlessly with his tusk.

Narsimha Avatar

In His fourth incarnation, Lord Vishnu appeared in the form of Narsimha (half-man, half-lion) to kill the king of the demons Hiranyakashipu, the elder brother of Hiranyaksha. He mourned the death of his brother, Hiranyaksha. Filled with revenge he swore to himself, "I will practise severe penance to obtain the boons and kill all the Gods."

He reached the mountains and performed strict austerities for years. Ant hills and grasses grew on him but he did not move. So intense was his penance that Brahma had to appear before him, "I am very pleased with your prayers, son. What is your wish?" The demon put forth his wish, "Neither at day nor at night, any man, beast, God or demon may kill me. No weapon or instrument, stone or wood may destroy me.

Indoors or outdoors, on Earth or in sky, nobody may harm me."

Brahma blessed him, "May it be so!" Becoming powerful thus, Hiranyakashipu proclaimed himself the Supreme God and asked everyone to worship him only. He also ordered to destroy all the idols of Gods. However, his son Prahlad was a great devotee of Lord Vishnu.

One day Hiranyakashipu lovingly asked his son, "Dear son, what do you think is the best thing in life?" Prahlad replied, "To renounce the world and seek refuge in Vishnu." Hiranyakashipu was shocked. He could not tolerate that his son loved his enemy Vishnu.

Annoyed, he sent him to an ashram meant for demons' children. There he was taught to worship Hiranyakashipu (his father) only. After completing education, when Prahlad returned to the palace, he again asked, "Now who is the greatest?" Prahlad answered, "O father! You have unnecessarily developed enmity against Vishnu.

If you wish well for yourself, you too should adore Him!" Hiranyakashipu's anger hit the roof. He thundered, "Throw this boy down from the mountain top." Prahlad was thrown down the mountain but he did'nt even get a scratch. Frustrated, the king started a series of tortures on Prahlad but Lord Vishnu saved him everytime.

Depressed, Hiranyakashipu went to his sister Holika for help. She had a boon that fire could not burn her. She was made to sit on a big bonfire, with Prahlad in her lap. The onlookers held their breath with anxiety, but when the fire extinguished they were amazed to see that Prahlad was safe, while Holika was burnt to ashes. Hiranyakashipu's fury was at its climax now. He

got an iron pillar heated and asked Prahlad to embrace it. Prahlad did not hesitate and embraced the pillar at once but to everyone's surprise, he was not burnt at all. With folding hands, he said, "Lord Vishnu is everywhere to save His devotees." At this, Hiranyakashipu rushed to hit him with his mace, "I am going to kill you this very moment.

Let Him come and save you." And he pounced upon the little Prahlad. With a thundering sound, the pillar cracked and Vishnu appeared in the form of Narsimha. He was half-man, half-lion with terrible teeth and sharp nails on His paws. He caught Hiranyakashipu and placed him on His thighs.

He sat on the threshold of the court-room, pierced His nails into his body and killed the demon on the spot. Hiranyakashipu's death did not violate any of the three conditions of the boon.

The time of his death was twilight— neither day nor night. He died on the threshold of his palace, which was neither inside nor outside, and his slayer was half-man, half-lion, therefore not a man, beast or God.

Narsimha then coronated Prahlad as the king in place of Hiranyakashipu. Thus, it was the triumph over evil and the establishment of virtue.

ष्इति सभगवान्कृत्वा विष्णुर्जज्जनितोदयं
कुशलमचलं प्रह्लादाय प्रदाय सहायुषा।
निजनिजपदे देवान्धृत्वा स्थिरस्थितिपालने
दमितमगमत्सौम्यां मूर्तिं विधाय सुधाम्बुधिम्।।

Thus Narsimha Avtar -Lord Vishnu, blessed Prahlad with undestructible life, all pervading peace; then directing all demigods in their respective positions for proper functioning of the universe, Lord proceeded to his peaceful disposition .

Vamana Avatar

Lord Vishnu, in His fifth incarnation, appeared as Vamana, a dwarf-Brahmin and attended King Bali's sacrifice. Bali was the grandson of Prahlad and the king of demons. He aspired to defeat Indra, the King of Heaven. So he performed the Vishwajit

Yajna to please Agni (the fire god).

Agni God blessed Bali, "Son, I am pleased with your prayers. Take this divine chariot, celestial weapons and a protective armour."

Bali took his divine chariot and set out to conquer the Heaven. Defeating Indra, he ascended the throne of Heaven and became the Lord of the three worlds.

Meanwhile in a hermitage, Aditi, the mother of Gods, could not bear the defeat of Indra and was very sad. She prayed ardently to Vishnu, "O Lord! Please restore my son's kingdom and His honour."

Lord Vishnu appeared, "O divine lady! Your prayers shall not prove fruitless. I shall be born as a son to you and protect your progeny."

So Lord Vishnu rein-carnated as a

dwarf— the Vamana. Clad in a loin cloth, He carried a staff of an ascetic in one hand and a water jug (kamandala) in the other. As the time came, Aditi requested her son, "Go and defeat Bali for the welfare of Gods and the human beings." Following His mother's advice, Vamana went to meet Bali, who had vowed to fulfil any wish of a Brahmin, no matter how difficult it might be.

Bali greeted Vamana warmly and said, "O holy man! What can I do for you? Ask for anything you desire." But Vamana kept quiet.

Seeing this Bali again said, "Do not hesitate, ask for whatever you want — cows, elephants, horses, chariots, villages... anything."

This time Vamana shook His head and said, "All I

need is a piece of land equal to my three steps."
Bali laughed aloud, "Why three steps! You are talking to mighty King Bali... It's your chance to ask for any riches."

But Vamana insisted, "No King! I only want the land, worth my three steps."

Bali laughed and mocked, "Okay, if you so insist then you shall have, what you want."
And to everybody's surprise, Vamana began to grow more and more. Bali and all others present, were astounded to see the whole creation of the dwarf's body.

Now Vamana began to measure the three paces. With His first step, He covered the whole Earth, and with His second step, He covered the Heaven.

Vamana now asked Bali, "You had promised me three paces of land. I have covered all that was yours in two steps. Where should I place my third step? You have failed to keep your word and for that you shall suffer."

Bali said, "O Lord! I am not afraid of punishment. Place your third step on my head. My word is more valuable to me than all my possessions put together."

So Vamana put His foot on Bali's head and pushed him down into the underworld (Patal Lok). Lord Indra was the King of Heaven again and ruled it with honour and dignity. All the other Gods too restored their lost glory.

इति स भगवान्विष्णुः कर्तं सुराश्रयिणी श्रियं
बलिभुजतरुच्छायाहीनान्विधाय महासुरान्।
अपि खलजनासंगाद्भूमेर्गतस्य तलं बलेः
प्रणयरचितां पुण्येः कीर्तिं निनाय समुन्नतिम्।।

Thus Vaman Avtar Lord Vishnu, in order to restore laxmi back to the demigods, freeing the Asuras from the strong shadows of tree like arms of Bali cruel though, recalling his virtues, Lord pushed Bali in the depths of the under-world.

Parsurama Avatar

In Tretayuga, the Kshatriyas became all powerful and were tyrannising everyone. To end all such evils, Lord Vishnu re-incarnated as Parsurama, the youngest son of Sage Jamadagni and his wife Renuka. Though a Brahmin, Parsurama had an inordinate love for weapons and His favourite weapon was the parsu (axe).

The parsu was a reward from Shiva, for His great penance and worship, and Parsurama was named after it.

Once when Parsurama and His brothers were away, a Kshatriya King, Kartavirya Arjuna entered their ashram with his army and forcefully took away their wish-fulfilling cow 'Kamdhenu'. Renuka and Jamadagni felt very sad on hearing the cries of their beloved cow.

When Parsurama returned, Renuka wept bitterly, "My son, what a misery! Our Kamdhenu has been taken away by the king's men." Parsurama stormed out carrying His axe. He attacked the king just as a lion attacks an elephant. After killing all his soldiers, He had a duel with the king. This king had one thousand arms so he released five hundred arrows together.

Parsurama immediately destroyed all the king's arrows. He then cut off his arms and threw him down a mountain peak. When the king's sons saw their father killed, they all fled in fear.

Parsurama returned home with Kamdhenu. But Jamadagni retorted, "You have commited a sin by killing the king. You should surrender yourself to Sri Krishna and go on a pilgrimage to atone this sin." Accepting his father's order, Parsurama visited the holy places for one year.

Once, Renuka went to the river to get some water for fire sacrifice and returned home very late.

Jamadagni was so angry that he ordered his sons, "Cut off her head as she has failed in her duty!" None of the sons came forward. He got furious. When Parsurama came he asked Him to kill His mother and His disobedient brothers.

Parsurama knew the power of His father's austerity, so He carried out his command at once.

Being very pleased, Jamadagni offered Him to make a wish. Parsurama requested, "I have two wishes, father — first, bring my innocent mother and brothers back to life; and second, that they would not remember having been killed by me." They all instantly came to life as if awakened from sound sleep.

On the other hand, Kartavirya Arjuna's sons were hankering for the revenge. While Parsurama was away, they invaded the ashram. They found Jamadagni deep in meditation and beheaded him. Renuka swooned on seeing this. When Parsurama came to know about it, He mourned the death of His father. Filled with grief and anger, He vowed, "I'll make the Earth devoid of the Kshatriyas and all their twenty-one generations."

With a terrible axe in His hand and the eyes blood-red with fury, He caught hold of all the sons of the king one after another and killed them. The existence of the Kshatriyas was wiped out from the surface of the globe. The country again smiled with peace and prosperity.

Then Parsurama conducted several yajnas to purify Himself and gifted the land He had acquired after killing the kings and princes, to the sages who had joined Him in the sacrifices.

Finally, He built a hermitage at the foot of the Mahendra Mountain and settled down for penance. It is believed that He still lives there as He is ageless.

Parsurama was one of the eight immortals (chiranjee-vies).

He was not only a great hero but also a learned person. He embodied several noble qualities. He did not kill married princes, women and those kings who performed religious sacrifices.

In the Ramayana, Parsurama came to the betrothal ceremony of the seventh Avatara, Rama, to the princess Sita. As a test of worthiness, the suitors were required to lift and string the bow of Shiva, given to the King Janaka

by Parsurama. Rama successfully strung the bow, but in the process it broke into two, producing a tremendous noise that reached the ears of Parsurama. When He arrived at the palace, the Kshatriyas were afraid to confront the sage, but Sita approached Him.

Parsurama blessed her, 'Saubhagyawati bhavah', literally meaning "Be thou blessed with good luck". So when He turned to confront Rama, the destroyer of Shiva's bow, He could not pick up His axe to do so, as He blessed Sita with good luck Himself. At the same time, He recognised Rama for what He truly was, namely, the Avatar of Vishnu. He also realised that His incarnation had come to an end and returned to His hermitage in the Mahendra Mountain. The Vishnu-effulgence of Parsurama merged itself with Rama's personality. Here is a popular verse in His memory—

अश्वत्थामा: बाली व्यासः हनुमानश्चः विभीषणः
कृपा परशुरामश्चः सप्तैते चिरंजीविनः।।

Ashwatthama, Bali, Vyasa, Hanuman, Vibhishana, Kripa and Parasurama- these are the seven eternal, ageless, immortal souls according to our traditional belief. In particular, it is believed Parasurama is sitting even today in penance at Mahendra Mountain. Why this great penance? Not for himself, but for the peace and happiness of the whole world

Rama Avatar

Lord Vishnu, in His seventh incarnation appeared on the Earth as Sri Rama. Rama was born as the eldest son of King Dashratha of Ayodhya. He is known as Maryada Purusottama (the perfect man) and is the emblem of righteousness.

Rama was the ideal husband who saved His wife

Sita, from Ravana, the King of Lanka. Sita is considered to be an Avatar of Lakshmi and the embodiment of perfect womanhood.

Ravana had obtained a boon from Brahma that he could not be defeated either by a demon or a man. Being powerful, he had become a devilish king.

Frustrated, Gods approached Vishnu and implored, "Lord! Save us from the terror of Ravana." So Vishnu in His Avatar as Rama, was born to teach mankind the importance of duty over desire.

King Dashratha of Ayodhya was blessed with four sons, as the outcome of 'Putrakameshti' yagya and the holy Payasa was thus consumed by the three queens— Kaushalya, Kaikaiy and Subhadra. Vishnu Avtara Rama was born to Kaushalya, Kaikaiy gave birth to Bharata and Subhadra gave birth lakshmana & Shatrughana. There were celebrations in whole Ayodhya. As growing young Princes Rama and

all His brothers learnt the warfare techniques from the family preceptor, Vashishtha. When they came of age, the Sage Vishwamitra took Rama and His brother Laxmana to the swayamvara ceremony of Sita. The challenge was to string the bow of Shiva, and shoot an arrow with it.

This task was considered impossible for any ordinary king or living being, as this was the personal weapon of Shiva, more powerful, holy and of divine creation than conceivable.

A large assembly of people was gathered to see the bow, as Lord Rama took it up in His hand. As, He bent the bow to string, it cracked in two pieces, making a thundering explosion which rendered all present unconscious, except for Vishwamitra, Rama and Laxmana. Rama was married to Sita, and His brothers to Sita's sisters with great fanfare. Ayodhya was decorated like a bride

to welcome all the princes with their wives. In between celebrations, Dashratha proclaimed Rama's coronation.

All except Manthara, the maid servant of Kaikeyi, were delighted at the news. She poisoned the ears of Kaikeyi,

"Now is the time to ask the two boons which Dashratha promised you in the battlefield; Bharat be coronated as the king and Rama be sent to the forest for fourteen years."

Influenced, Kaikeyi took offence and demanded the two boons from Dashratha. Helpless and grieved, Dashratha conceded. For the sake of His father's honour, Rama accepted the proposal happily.

When Sita heard about the exile, she pleaded before Rama, "If you must go to the forest, then I shall walk in front of you and smoothen your path by crushing the thorns under my feet. I wish to be by your side at all times." Laxmana too insisted to go along, and Lord Rama had to agree. Unable to bear separation from his beloved son, Dashratha passed away after Rama left.

Rama, Laxmana and Sita wandered from one forest to the other and finally settled in a small hut in Panchvati.

Meanwhile, the king of Lanka, Ravana heard about the beauty of Sita and plotted an evil plan to kidnap her.

He ordered a demon Maricha, to disguise as a golden deer and take Rama away from the hut. Maricha had no option but to agree.

Sita was enamoured at the sight of the golden deer wandering in front of their hut, "What a beautiful golden deer! Lord, please catch it for me."

Rama replied, "A deer as you explained, can only be an illusion or a demon. Don't fool yourself, Sita." But Sita did not agree.

With great reluctance, Rama left instructing Laxmana, "Take care of Sita while I go chasing the deer."

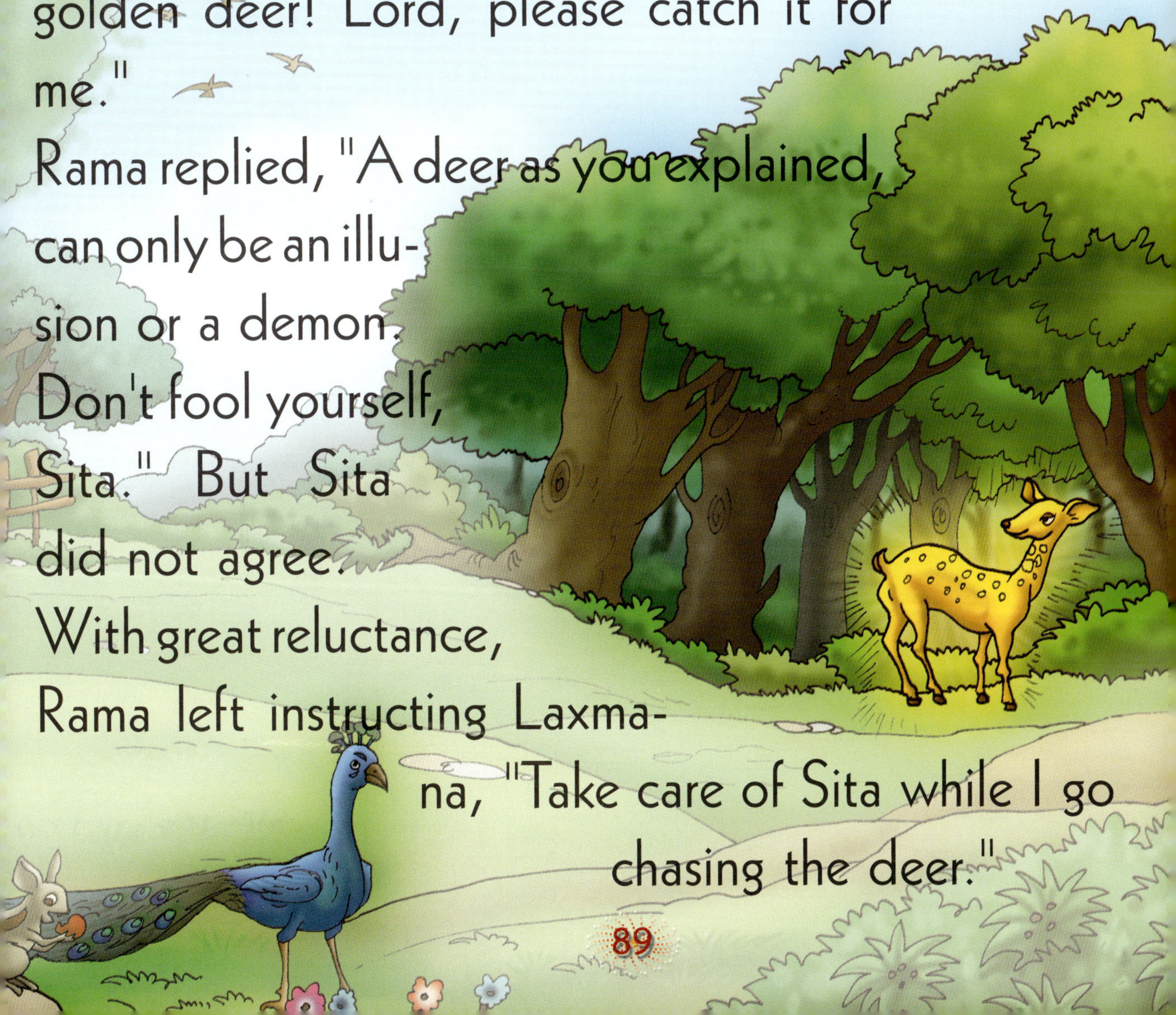

After some time, Rama's cry echoed in the forest. Upon hearing it, Sita got worried. She requested Laxmana to help his brother, Rama.

Laxmana first hesitated, then relenting, drew a line of protection (Laxman Rekha) and asked Sita not to cross it.

Seizing this opportunity, Ravana appeared as a saint and kidnapped her. When Rama and Laxmana returned, they found Sita missing. Grief-stricken, they began the desperate search to discover where Sita had been taken. After traversing a distance in many directions, they came across the magical eagle Jatayu, who was dying. Jatayu told them, "Oh Lord! A demon Ravana was flying away with a crying, struggling Sita towards the south. I had flown to her rescue, but the demon was too powerful for me."

Saying so, Jatayu died in Rama's arms. Rama was overcome with love and affection for the bird which sacrificed its own life for Sita.

He decided, "I must confront wicked Ravana and his empire." Both the brothers went southwards and met Hanuman and his master, Sugreeva. Sugreeva had been deceived by his own brother, Bali. On hearing his story Rama promised, "I will help you kill cruel Bali

and get back the throne of Kishkindha." In return, Sugreeva also assured , "Lord, I will help you find Mother Sita."

In due course, Rama kept His promise and Sugreeva sent his Vanara-Sena to help Rama locate Sita. Devoted to Rama, Hanuman exerted himself greatly over the search for Sita. He was the first to discover Sita in the Ashok Vatika. Handing over Rama's ring to her, he conveyed Lord Rama's message, "Lord Rama will arrive here soon and set you free after defeating Ravana."

Rama and Sugreeva's Vanara-sena built a miraculous bridge of floating stones across the ocean and entered Lanka under the very nose of the wicked Ravana. There ensued a fierce battle, in which great heroes from both sides fought to death, day after day.

One by one, great demons such as Kumbhakarna, Narantaka and Indrajit, the son of Ravana, fell before the unlimited powers of Hanuman, Laxmana, Sugreeva and Rama. Finally, Ravana came to the battlefield in his chariot.

He used deadly weapons against Rama and Laxmana but none of them could hurt them with truth and justice on their side. The battle between Rama and Ravana ensued for long.

It was becoming difficult to defeat Ravana as he was fighting in his air-borne chariot. Suddenly, Indra appeared, "Rama, take my celestial chariot. It will help you defeat Ravana." Driven by Matali, the chariot took Rama up, up, up in the air.

But as Rama's arrows pierced through Ravana's heads, another one appeared.

Rama was puzzled, "I must use Brahmastra to kill this ten-headed Ravana." Brahmastra was handed over by Lord Brahma, and passed from sage to sage. Rama closed His eyes, chanted a mantra and charged the weapon. The weapon pierced through Ravana's navel and he fell dead instantly.

Rama and Sita were reunited. Along with Laxmana, they returned to Ayodhya amidst universal rejoicing.

There, Rama was crowned king and ruled for many years in peace and prosperity.

Through Rama's example, Vishnu wanted to portray the qualities that make up an ideal man.

नीलाम्बुज श्यामकोमलाड्.ग सीतासमारोपितवामभागम्।
पार्णो महासायकचारुचापम् नमामि रामं रघुवंशनाथं।।

Lord Rama is the chief amongst the Raghus. His handsome body is of dark blue colour like the blue lotus. He has Sita seated on his left. He is the one, who wields beautiful bow and arrows in his hands. I bow to such great Lord!

Krishna Avatar

Krishna appeared in the Dwaparyuga along with His elder brother, Balrama. Krishna is worshipped as the source of all other Avatars, including Vishnu.

The Kingdom of Mathura was once ruled by a wicked and cruel king, Kansa. Kansa had ascended the throne by imprisoning his own father, Ugrasena.

Depressed of his tyranny, Mother Earth complained to Lord Brahma, "I cannot bear the burden of the wicked king anymore. He is great enemy of justice, morality and nobility."

Brahma prayed to Lord Vishnu who assured Him, "O Lord! Please don't worry, soon I will take birth as Krishna, and kill wicked Kansa."

During the marriage of his sister, Devki with Vasudeva, Kansa heard an echoing prophesy from Heaven, "Kansa! Your end is at hand. The eighth son born to Devki will be your slayer!"

At this, Kansa drew his sword to kill Devki right then, but Vasudeva begged, "Please spare her, I promise you to surrender our eighth son." Kansa imprisoned the couple in a stone dungeon.

Thereafter, he mercilessly killed six of Devki's sons as soon as they were born. Her seventh son, Balrama was saved from a similar fate. While still unborn, he was transported with divine help, from his mother's womb to the womb of Rohini, Vasudeva's second wife, who lived in Gokul.

Later at midnight, amidst a raging storm, Devki's eighth son was born. And then a series of miracles happened. The prison door unlocked and as the guards fell in deep slumber, Vasudeva walked out of the prison carrying Krishna on his head. He crossed the Yamuna River and reached Gokul, where he found Yashoda sleeping with a baby girl.

Vasudeva exchanged babies and returned to the prison. When Kansa heard that Devki's eighth child had been born, he rushed to the prison. He seized the baby girl, but she slipped from his hands and flew into the sky saying, "Wicked Kansa, I am Mahamaya. Your destroyer is another one, alive and well, in Gokul."

Kansa was shell-shocked. He ordered his soldiers to kill each and every new born baby.

Then he went to Putna, an ogress, and ordered, "Kill all the babies born on the same day when Devki gave birth to the baby." Putna poisoned Krishna with her breast milk. But baby Krishna suckled so hard, that with a scream of agony, she fell to the ground and died.

Little Krishna thus, became popular.

One of His favourite pranks was to steal butter and eat it with His friends. Because of this, He was affectionately called Makhan Chor (the butter thief). When the cowherd girls (gopis) would go to the river to fetch water, Krishna and His friends would reach their house, to steal curd and butter. When the gopis complained, Krishna always used to hide in Yashoda's lap.

A beautiful gopi, Radha, was very fond of Krishna's music. She danced to the tunes of His flute. Evil Kansa conspired devilish plans one after the other to kill Krishna, and every time Krishna killed his enemies. He killed Trinavarta, the wind demon and Aghasura, a demon in the form of a gigantic snake, who swallowed Krishna and His cowherd boy friends.

Krishna also punished Kaliya, a many-hooded serpent. This snake had poisoned the water of Yamuna river. Krishna danced on his head and eventually the Kaliya snake surrendered to him, "Please forgive me, O Lord! I will go from here." Such were the adventures of Krishna during His childhood.

With an intention to teach Indra a lesson one day, Krishna advised His father, "Stop worshiping Indra.

Instead worship Govardhan Hill."

With great hesitation, Nanda did this and annoyed Indra greatly, "I will punish you for stopping my worship."

Saying so, Indra sent torrential rains to drown His defaulters. Fearing Pralaya, everyone begged Krishna for help. Krishna lifted the Govardhan Hill on His little finger and the residents of Vrindavan sought refuge under it.

Finally, the time had come for Krishna to relieve His parents from the clutches of evil Kansa. He went to Mathura along with Balrama. There He strangled Kansa and his eight brothers to death, and restored the throne of Mathura to its rightful King Ugrasena.

Krishna became Arjuna's charioteer during the battle of (Kurukshetra) and gave the world the timeless wisdom of Gita.

वसुदेवसुतं देवं कंस चाणूरमर्दनम्।
देवकी परमानन्दं कृष्णंम् वन्दे जगद्गुरुम्।।

Krishna is the Supreme Lord, Son of Devaki and Vasudeva. He is the slayer of Kansa and Chanur. I bow to such great lord and may god bless me with his grace always!

Buddha Avatar

Buddha is considered to be the ninth incarnation of Lord Vishnu. Siddhartha Gautama was given this title after He found enlightenment under a Bodhi tree at Bodh Gaya.

Siddhartha was born in Lumbini, to Kosala King Suddhodana. At birth celebrations, the hermit seer Asita journeyed from his mountain abode

and announced, "This child would either become a great king (chakravartin) or a holy man." King Suddhodana wanted his son to be a great king. So he ordered his ministers, "Give my son all the comforts of a royal palace. Keep him away from any kind of religious teachings or knowledge of human suffering."

At the age of sixteen, his father arranged his marriage to Yasodhara who, in due time, gave birth to a son, Rahula. One day, Gautama thought, "I have led a luxurious life but I think, material wealth is not the ultimate goal of life."

Wishing to survey the condition of his subjects, he left the palace. There he saw four sights which he had never seen before – an old man, a crippled man, a decaying corpse (death) and an ascetic. Depressed, he came back with a heavy heart and started thinking – "How to over-come these sorrows of life?"

At the age of twenty nine, Gautama left his palace. It is said that, 'the horse's hooves were muffled by the Gods' to prevent guards from knowing the Bodhisatwa's departure. This event is known as 'The Great Departure'.

Gautama shaved off his head and put on yellow robes. Then he went to Rajgriha and started begging for alms in the street.

He practised severe Tapas (austerities) and Pranayama (practice of breath control) for six years. After asceticism and concentrating on meditation, he is said to have discovered what Buddhists call the Middle Way—a path of moderation, away from the extremes of self-indulgence and self-mortification. Then, sitting under a pipal tree, now known as the Bodhi tree, he vowed never to arise until he had found the Truth.

After forty-nine days of meditation, at the age of thiry-five, He attained Enlightenment. From then on, He was known as the Buddha or 'The Enlightened One'.

At the age of eighty, sensing that His end was near, He made His last journey to Kusinagar, Mallas. He reached a grove of sal trees which were flowering out of season and there lay down for his last rest on Earth. It was there that Buddha's soul entered into Nirvana.

बुद्धम् शरणम् गच्छामिः
धम्मम् शरणम् गच्छामिः।
संघम् शरणम् गच्छामिः

I bow to Buddha and resort to him as refuge.
I take refuge in reality (religion, duty).
I take refuge in the community.

Kalki Avatar

The tenth and the last incarnation of Lord Vishnu is Kalki, who will come riding a white horse and carrying a drawn sword blazing like a comet. Kalki will accomplish the final destruction of the wicked and prepare for the renewal of creation and the resurgence of virtue in the next Mahayuga. Kalki will

come, when men will forget the name of the God and no longer offer Yajna to the Gods. The Gods will go to Brahma to seek a solution.

Brahma will advise them to seek help from Vishnu. Vishnu will then ascend to Earth in the form of Kalki to solve the problems of Kaliyuga. He will rid the world of all wicked kings and false prophets. After the defeat and destruction of evil

on Earth, the Satyayuga (Golden Age) will begin. Kalki will divide the Earth into earthly kingdoms among His generals, then perform the Ashwamedha and Rajasuya sacrifices for the Gods. Sumati and Vishnuyasha, His parents, will then travel to the holy place of Badrikashram, where they will live until their death.

After the siring of Kalki's sons, He will reign on Earth for thousand years as the King of Shambha-la. Having finished His mission of restoring peace, Kalki will return to Vaikuntha.

तस्मिन्काले निरालोके पापतमापेदये। उत्पत्स्यतेर्कसंकाशः शिशुः कर्किकुले द्विजः।।
विष्णुर्भूभारशान्त्यर्थी सोथ विष्णुयशाः क्षितौ। चरिष्यत्यश्वमारुह्य म्लेच्छसंक्षयदीक्षितः।।

Then omni virtuous Lord Vishnu, always willing to release the burden and restore peace of Mother earth, destroying the evil, reincarnated as Kalki will go around the world riding on a horse.

Activities

Let's do some fun activities

Match the following by drawing lines. The first one has been done for you.

Rama	Hiranyakashipu
Krishna	Hiranyaksha
Vamana	Ravana
Narsimha	Gautama Buddha
Varaha	Kansa
Siddhartha	Bali

The following pictures remind you of some events. Write the names of the events in proper boxes given below.

1

2

3

4

5

6

1

2

3

4

5

6

Join the dots and colour the picture.
Try to identify it.

Here are the pictures of ten avatars of Vishnu. Arrange them chronologically according to their occurrence on Earth.

1